D0905441

## From The Baroque To The 20th Century

# *Classical Duets for All*

## Playable on ANY TWO INSTRUMENTS
### or any number of instruments in ensemble

### WILLIAM RYDEN

## TABLE OF CONTENTS

## INSTRUMENTATION

EL96127 - Piano/Conductor, Oboe
EL96128 - Flute, Piccolo
EL96129 - B♭ Clarinet, Bass Clarinet
EL96130 - Alto Saxophone
    (E♭ Saxes and E♭ Clarinets)
EL96131 - Tenor Saxophone
EL96132 - B♭ Trumpet, Baritone T.C.

EL96133 - Horn in F
EL96134 - Trombone,
    Baritone B.C., Bassoon, Tuba
EL96135 - Violin
EL96136 - Viola
EL96137 - Cello/Bass
EL96138 - Percussion

Editor: Thom Proctor
Cover: Dallas Soto

# ALPHABETICAL CONTENTS

**WILLIAM RYDEN** was born in New York City and is a life-long resident of Forest Hills, New York. He received his advanced musical training at The American Conservatory of Music in Chicago and at the Mannes College of Music in New York. The diversity of his composing ranges from solos to orchestra works, in both vocal and instrumental music. Since 1982 he has received 25 grants from the Meet-the-Composer Foundation. His numerous compositions and arrangements have been published by various prominent educational and performance music publishers.

# ARIA
## from "Rigoletto"

**VIOLIN**

GIUSEPPE VERDI
(1813-1901)

4

# AU CLAIR DE LA LUNE

JEAN BAPTISTE LULLY
(1632-1687)

Andante con moto

# LULLABY
## Opus 49, No. 4

JOHANNES BRAHMS
(1833-1897)

# SICILIENE

JACQUES AUBERT
(1689-1753)

# DUETTO

IGNACE PLEYEL
(1757-1831)

# MINUET
## in C Minor, BWV Anh. 121

JOHANN SEBASTIAN BACH
(1685-1750)

# MELODY
## Album for the Young, Opus 68, No. 1

ROBERT SCHUMANN
(1810-1856)

# ALLEGRO
## K. 487

WOLFGANG AMADEUS MOZART
(1756-1791)

**Allegro**

# LARGHETTO
## from Six Canonic Sonatas

GEORG PHILIPP TELEMANN
(1681-1767)

# PAVANA

ALESSANDRO SCARLATTI
(1660-1725)

# DUET

"The Magic Flute", K. 620

WOLFGANG AMADEUS MOZART
(1756-1791)

# TWO ADAGIOS
## 1.
### Sonata No. 2

ARCANGELO CORELLI
(1653-1713)

# 2.
## Sonata No. 3

# MINUET IN CANON
## K. 94

WOLFGANG AMADEUS MOZART
(1756-1791)

**Allegro moderato**

# TWO RIGAUDONS

JEAN PHILIPPE RAMEAU
(1683-1764)

# LOST IS MY QUIET
## (1691)

HENRY PURCELL
(1659-1695)

**Andante con moto**

# ECHO
## Hob. II, No. 39

JOSEPH HAYDN
(1732-1809)

**Allegro con brio**

*For best results players should stand far apart.

# CAPRICHO CATALAN

## España, Opus 165

ISAAC ALBENIZ
(1860-1909)